THE
Archive Photographs
SERIES

LONG ASHTON
AND
LEIGH WOODS

Wilfred and Nell Kempe. Wilfred was proprietor of Kempe's School, Long Ashton, from c. 1874 to 1914.

THE
Archive Photographs
SERIES

LONG ASHTON
AND
LEIGH WOODS

Compiled by
The Long Ashton Local History Society
and
SCALA
(Society for Conservation at Long Ashton)

CHALFORD

The Chalford Publishing Company
St Mary's Mill, Chalford,
Stroud, Gloucestershire, GL6 8NX

ISBN 0 7524 1027 X

Typesetting and origination by
The Chalford Publishing Company
Printed in Great Britain by
Bailey Print, Dursley, Gloucestershire

Cover picture:
C. Cole, Eldred Walker (Man o' Mendip) and Bob Hathaway
at Long Ashton Cider Institute. (*See Chapter 10: The Research Station*)

Acknowledgements

We would like to thank the Bristol United Press, Bromhead Photography, the *Clevedon Mercury, The Field* (photographer, Leslie F. Thompson), Long Ashton Research Station, North Somerset Museum Service, and Peter Watts for their kind permission to reproduce their photographs. We are also indebted to the following people who have kindly loaned us their photographs: Mrs V. Atherton, Mrs J. Avery, Miss B. Barnes, Mr H. Butler, Miss P. Chorley, Mr R. Chorley, Mrs G. Cook, Mrs B. Cross, Mrs B. Fraser, Mrs Y. Gover, Mrs D. Harris, Mr W. Harris, Mrs V. Hopton, Mr and Mrs B. Huish, Mr and Mrs J. Kingston, Mr R. Kingston, Mr M. James, Mrs M. Magro, Dr M. Marston, Mr W. Perry, Mrs V. Taylor, Mrs E. Wright and Mr and Mrs D. Yeo, and to all those who assisted with factual information and verification. We sincerely apologise if we have inadvertently omitted anyone from the above list.

Contents

Introduction

There is evidence that people lived in the district in prehistoric times. Roman coins have been found in the area and there was a large Roman settlement at Gatcombe, just outside the village but within the parish boundary. Long Ashton began to develop in Saxon times and during the reign of Edward the Confessor (1042-66) it was held by three thanes. The name is Saxon in origin, too. In the Domesday survey of 1086, it is called Estune, which is usually interpreted as 'the settlement by the ash tree'. There were numerous ways of spelling the name, for example, Axston in 1244, Aysshton in 1391 and Ayscheton in 1503. Later, the prefix was added so it was written Lange Asshton in 1421 and Longeassheton in 1507. There were a number of small settlements such as the one near the church and Hobwell, at Yanley, Lamington and Kencot, which eventually linked together and this may be the reason why the prefix came to be used. The name is certainly very descriptive of the modern village. It has also been suggested that it is derived from Lyons Ashton. One of the several manors in the locality was more usually known as Ashton Lyons. In the mid-nineteenth century, Long Ashton was often just called 'Ashton'.

Estune was granted to Bishop Geoffrey of Coutances after the Norman Conquest in 1066. He kept some of the lands and granted the remainder to two sub-tenants, Roger the Bursar and Guy the Priest. There was a church here and about 30 acres of its land were held by a priest. Various families then held lands in the parish and eventually, the manors of Ashton Lyons, Ashton Meriets, Ashton Philips, Ashton Theynes and the Manor of the Parsonage were established. Except for the Manor of the Parsonage, each took its name from a family which at one time held land. The manors did not have strict boundaries and some of their lands were scattered about the parish. From 1285, the de Lyons family held the manor which bore their name. It then passed to a cousin and in 1454 was purchased by Richard Choke of Stanton Drew. Sir Richard is buried in a fine tomb in All Saints' Church with his second wife, Margaret.

In 1545, John Smyth, who like other prosperous Bristol merchants had begun to invest in land, purchased the manor. The following year, he bought the Manor of Ashton Meriets, the rectory and the advowson of the parish church and by 1603 the Smyth family had become the principal landowners in the parish. Ashton Court and its owners were to play an important part in village life until the middle of the present century. Sir John Smyth, who died in 1741, left the estates to three of his sisters – Anne, Florence (the wife of Jarrit Smith, a Bristol lawyer) and Arabella (the wife of Edward Gore). Sir John had been heavily in debt to Jarrit, who now took Ashton Court and the park in settlement. Jarrit also held one third of the remainder of the estates through Florence, his wife. He later purchased Arabella's share from her son. Anne left her third share of the estates to her nephew. Eventually Jarrit Smith was made a baronet and was given the right to use the Smyth coat of arms. Heavy death duties eventually brought about the end of the estates. Some farms were sold after Dame Emily's death to help pay death duties but when Esmé died in 1946, her grandson, Lt. Commander Greville Adrian Cavendish, the new owner of Ashton Court, was forced to sell the remaining estates. It was the end of an era for Long Ashton which had spanned four centuries.

Farm work had long been the main occupation but there were various other forms of employment. There had been a fulling mill at Gatcombe in 1378 and, in 1735, a paper mill was operating there. By 1815, together with mills at Kencot and Bower walls, it produced snuff. A mustard, annato (a dye) and drug mill was located there in 1846. Kencot was a flour and corn mill in the 1830s but, by 1861, it had been replaced by an iron foundry, which was operated until about 1920. Ashton Court offered work on its Home Farm at Bower Ashton for gamekeepers, foresters, carpenters and other estate workers. Women were mostly employed in domestic work, a few at the mansion and others in the large houses in the locality. Laundry work was a thriving cottage industry and there were two commercial laundries in the parish. The Sunlight Laundry opened at the former New Inn, Rownham some time after 1891 and closed in the 1920s. The Fenswood Steam Laundry operated from about 1891 to 1914.

Seventeenth-century indentures granted rights to quarry stone for lime-burning. There was a small quarry near the present Long Ashton golf course which supplied stone for the building of Church House and the almshouses and at another one, near the top of Providence Lane, stone was obtained for road-making and maintenance. There is still a large working quarry in Longwood Lane. In 1655, lead was smelted near the wood below Stokeleigh and the site was taken over for copper-smelting around 1720. Coal was mined locally from at least the eighteenth century with some seams stretching back under the village towards Nailsea. At one time, the Ashton Vale Company considered sinking a shaft between the Research Station and Cambridge Batch. Many villagers were employed in the pits and were able to walk across the fields to work. The last pit in the Bedminster/Ashton area closed in 1924. Between 1858 and 1873, iron ore varying from 600 to 3,000 tons a year was extracted from the hill north-west of Providence which is still called 'the Iron Plantation'. Work continued until the First World War. The ore was sent to Bristol for smelting. Skids had to be placed on the wheels of the wagons which carried the loads of ore down the hill. These made ruts in the road and the neighbourhood was red with dust from the ore.

Nowadays, there is limited local employment and most people commute into Bristol or the surrounding district to work. Originally, the only links with Bristol were via Rownham ferry or through Bedminster. The ferry was moved upstream when the docks were modernised, and it finally closed in the early 1930s when alternative routes came into use. Communications had improved greatly with the construction of the turnpike roads in the eighteenth century but travelling was still very dangerous. In 1788, Rev John Collinson fought off a robber who stopped him in Rownham Lane and tried to seize his horse's bridle. The opening of the Clifton Suspension Bridge in 1864 provided yet another route into Bristol but the Ashton Swing Bridge did not open until 1906. The first motor-bus to serve the village ran from Hotwells to Birdwell the following year.

When it became known, in 1862, that development of the Leigh Woods area was being considered, the Leigh Woods Land Company was formed, in order to ensure that the scenic beauty of the area would be preserved. In 1865, Sir Greville Smyth sold 168 acres at Leigh Woods to the Land Company. About 60 acres were set apart for ornamental purposes, 20 acres for roads, leaving about eight acres to be divided into building plots. The land south of Nightingale Valley had been fully developed by 1909. Burwalls was destroyed by the development and it was feared that the same would happen to Stokeleigh Camp. Mr G.A. Wills purchased 80 acres at Nightingale Valley and part of Hanging Woods from the Land Company and gave them to the National Trust. Mr Melville Wills gave a further 63½ acres to the Trust in 1933 and the Misses Wills added just under five acres on a very long lease. In about 1949, Mrs Wynne Willson and Mrs E. Eberle gave ten acres, comprising the remainder of Hanging Woods, to the Trust.

Long Ashton has had connections with a number of well-known people over the years. Dr Henry Mills Grace, father of W.G. Grace, the famous cricketer, was born at the Firs in 1808. His mother, Elizabeth, ran a small private school there. Robert Southey, Poet Laureate (1814-43), wrote of 'the beautiful vale of Ashton, the place of all others which I remember with most feeling'. The Hills, his mother Margaret's family, had lived here for generations until his grandfather built a new house at Bedminster. Southey's father, two of his brothers, three sisters and his cousin Margaret are all buried in Long Ashton churchyard, although the grave is no longer marked. Also buried here are members of Beverley Nichol's family, including his brother

Paul, who was born at the Mead. Beverley was born at the Woodlands, a large house in Bower Ashton. Although Leigh Woods had its own church from 1892, there is no graveyard, so some of its former residents are buried in Long Ashton churchyard, including Joseph Leech, newspaper proprietor and author of *Rural Rides*; Emma Marshall, the Victorian novelist, as well as members of the well-known Harvey family.

The Long Ashton Parish Council held its first meeting in the Parochial Schools on 14 December 1894. The 11 members had been elected to represent a range of interests in the parish. Thomas Dyke, the Estate Steward to Sir Greville Smyth, represented land interests; a doctor, a builder/postmaster and a tanner represented professions and trades; two farmers, an engine-wright, a coal-miner, a labourer and one of the estate workers represented labour interests while a retired solicitor from Leigh Woods represented residents' interests. At their first meeting, members of the Parish Council passed a resolution calling on Somerset Council to oppose the Bristol boundary extension proposals. They appear to have been unsuccessful as a small part of the parish was transferred to Bristol in 1898. In 1951, the whole of Bower Ashton and the area to the rear of Kings Head Lane became part of Bristol, as did the Ashton Vale Trading Estate, in 1966. Further boundary changes in 1980 transferred a small area at the western end of the parish, to Flax Bourton. This included Farleigh Hospital, formerly the Bedminster Union workhouse.

The leisurely pace of the horse and cart eventually gave way to the motor-car and heavy lorries. The main roads from Bristol to Weston-super-Mare and Clevedon passed through the village and further housing development this century led to ever more traffic. By the 1950s, the problem had become acute with an estimated 1,300 vehicles per hour passing through the village in each direction at peak times. Even crossing the road was becoming a major problem. Traffic often came to a complete standstill when holidaymakers were returning to Bristol, especially when a bank holiday coincided with the North Somerset Show at Ashton Court. Villagers often walked to the main road on bank holiday evenings to watch the traffic and count the number of coaches passing by. The opening of the Long Ashton bypass on 6 December 1968 restored peace to the village but unfortunately, the volume of traffic along the main road has again increased in recent years.

Limited development was allowed before the Second World War but the Smyth Estate kept a close eye on what was taking place. At one time, only Berberis hedges were allowed in Chestnut and Ridgeway Roads and a few remain to this day. Stone walls are still a distinctive feature along the main road. Covenants were put on some houses which were built on Smyth Estate land, stipulating, for example, that the property could only be used as a dwelling-house or a school, and that the purchaser must not be a Roman Catholic. The disposal of the Ashton Court estates transferred much property and land into private hands and opened the floodgates to developers. Between 1947 and 1994, 1,033 houses were built in Long Ashton, 272 of them on the Birdwell Estate between 1958 and 1961 and 155 at Westleaze/Ashton Theynes between 1978 and 1984.

There are 80 properties in the parish listed as being of special architectural or historic interest. These include Ashton Court mansion, and part of the Clifton Suspension Bridge, both of which are Grade I; All Saints' Church, some tombs in the churchyard, Gatcombe Court and the Chapel at Lower Court Farm, all Grade II*. The remainder are listed Grade II.

The photographs in this book show the parish of Long Ashton and Leigh Woods and its people from the late nineteenth century to the 1950s. Many changes have taken place during this period but, despite its close proximity to the City of Bristol, Long Ashton has managed to retain its separate identity.

One

Village Life (I)

We start with a selection of photographs from the late nineteenth and early twentieth centuries showing some of the inhabitants and part of the eastern end of the village. In the nineteenth century the main road was called Ashton Street. Long Ashton was still a very rural community, most of which belonged to the Ashton Court Estate. Most of the houses fronted the main road near the sites of ancient hamlets and there were small settlements at Yanley and Providence. The origins of some houses, especially those near the church, can be traced back to medieval times. Other large properties in the village date back to the eighteenth and nineteenth centuries and some of these were occupied by prosperous Bristolians, especially merchants, who found Long Ashton a pleasant place in which to reside. The photographs of Glebe Road remind us that changes were taking place and more were to come.

Lower Court Farm, 1880. Originally the manor-house of the manor of Ashton Philips, now only the east wing remains. By 1502, the manor was owned by Richard Ameryke, one of two Port of Bristol customs officers who, in 1488 and 1489, paid John Cabot £20, which Henry VII awarded him. Local tradition says that Cabot named America after him. Beside the house is the former chapel dating back to 1265.

Ernest Board lived at Bowley House, Short Lane, now No. 6 Hillside Road. In 1906 he painted his famous picture 'John Cabot's Departure for the Discovery of America in 1497'. It is now in the Bristol City Art Gallery.

Frank Cobbett with a penny-farthing bicycle. He was a member of the church choir and married Avena Blackburne, the daughter of Rev Gilbert Blackburne. They moved to Budleigh Salterton where their money ran out, leaving them quite poor in the latter part of their lives.

M.M. Stock and Harry Stock outside Ashover in 1872. The house was called The Cottage when William Ravenhill Stock and his wife moved there in February 1863. William Stock was a keen amateur photographer and took many of the early photographs of Long Ashton and district. He faced financial ruin after the loss of a cargo of sugar in 1883 and moved to Chelvey, then to Walton. He died in Clevedon in August 1907. Ashover is now a retirement home.

Sunnymead, 1909, looking towards the church. There has been a house here since 1403 when William Kyngton made an agreement to build a house of one bay. It was first called Kyngton's, later Church Cross Tenement. William Gough, a merchant, who lived here from 1840, laid out the knot-garden of dwarf box-hedges. Part of the present house dates back to the seventeenth and eighteenth centuries.

The Bridge, Yanley Lane, 1908, looking towards Long Ashton Road.

The top of Yanley Lane in summer 1908. Three people with a horse and cart climb up towards the main road. Two servants from one of the large houses nearby, pose for the photographer.

Boys walking home from school in 1905 pause by the bridge in Westleaze, near the entrance to Lower Court Farm. Percy Yeo is second on the left. Lower Court was approached by a path which led across the field to a double gate on the main road between the Mead and Church House. When Glebe Road was built, leading into Yanley Lane, this offered a better route. Development of the Westleaze/Ashton Theynes estate began here in 1978.

Glebe Road, 1913. A pair of semi-detached cottages, Nos. 8/10 and 12/14, were built at the top of the road in 1912 for senior workers of the Ashton Court Estate. Development progressed during the 1930s and more houses were built in 1953.

Nos. 100-108 Long Ashton Road, *c.* 1900. The post office moved across the road from Beaufort Cottage to No. 2 Long Ashton Road probably in the late nineteenth century. It moved again to this, the third site near the Ashton Arms. The Ashton Arms sign can just be seen in the background. (*See page 60*)

Florence and Emmie Hicks, carrying washing to Providence. Laundry work was an important occupation here for nearly 100 years and in 1881 95 laundresses were recorded in Long Ashton. The largest clusters were in Yanley Lane, Birdwell, Providence, and Archgrove. Produce was taken by horse and cart into Bristol and laundry brought back, for return later in the week. Some people can still remember the hillsides being white with washing.

Two

Ashton Court

Ashton Court stands on the site of an earlier manor-house belonging to the de Lyons family who were lords of the manor in the thirteenth and fourteenth centuries. The manor was known as Ashton Lyons, after the family name. In 1393, Thomas de Lyons was granted a licence by Richard II to enclose land to make a deer park. The house was much enlarged by Richard Choke, who became the owner in 1454. John Smyth, a Bristol merchant, purchased the manor and house in 1545. During the following centuries, the Smyths altered and enlarged the house. Dame Emily Smyth's daughter, Esmé, who inherited the estates from her mother in 1914, changed her name from Irby to Smyth and is remembered as the Hon. Mrs Esmé Smyth. When Esmé died in 1946, crippling death duties led to the disposal of the estate. The house lay unoccupied for some years until Bristol Corporation acquired the mansion and surrounding parkland in 1959. Refurbishment of the house began in 1974 and part of the building is now used for functions. There is now a small visitors' centre and the deer-park has also been re-established.

The West Front, Ashton Court, 1866. The mansion is a Grade I listed building.

Lower Lodge is sometimes called the Bristol Lodge or the Grass Lodge. Both Lower and Upper, i.e. Clarkencombe Lodge are shown on a map of 1826. The driveway from the Lower Lodge ran along behind the Coach and Horses (now the Smyth Arms) public house and then swung round to the front entrance of the house.

Gateway from Ashton Court in the 1860s. This was used by the Smyth family when they attended Long Ashton parish church. It was later replaced by Church Lodge.

Church Lodge, *c.* 1872. This lodge replaced the gateway shown in the previous photograph. Avena Blackburne, the vicar's daughter, wrote as a caption: 'New Lodge near the Church. First used by the Bishop Lord Arthur Harvey on the way to reopen the Church. Aug. 13 1872'.

The coachman at the entrance to Ashton Court in 1906 is Mr Traylor who lived in Upper Lodge. The butler standing at the rear of the carriage is Mr Webb. Seated in the carriage is the Hon. Mrs Esmé Irby whose signature appears on the photograph.

Sir Greville Smyth and party leaving Ashton Court for the Bristol races. John Henry Greville Upton (1836-1901) was a minor when he inherited the Ashton Court Estates and they were administered by his uncle, Mr Arthur Way. Greville assumed the family name of Smyth. He celebrated his coming of age on 2 January 1857.

Group in the Winter Gardens at Ashton Court, *c.* 1910. The central courtyard was converted into the Winter Gardens in 1885. It had an unusual cast-iron glazed roof which was later dismantled by Bristol City Council and the parts numbered with a view to re-erecting the structure in the future. Back row, second from right, is Sir Greville Smyth. Middle row, seated far right, is Dame Emily Smyth, while seated, third from the right, is the Hon. Mrs Esmé Irby.

The Garden Staff at Ashton Court, early 1900s. From left to right, back row: Charlie Beecham, W. Chamberlayne, Bill Bartlett, ? Bill Saunders, Frank Radford, Jim Pope, Joe Fisher (father). Middle row: -?-, Joby Ball, Bobby Hynam, Jim Carpenter, -?-, Harry Bridle (father), Albert Ball, Bill Oatway, Charlie Powell, Billy, Billy. Front row: -?-, T. Ambrose, -?-, Mr Draper (with dog), Mr Noble (head gardener), -?-, -?-, Mr Williams, Jack Ashley.

Mr Thomas Dyke and Miss Avena Blackburne standing outside the Ashton Court estate office. Thomas Dyke was Agent for the Ashton Court Estate from 1870 to about 1901. The estate office is now a private house and the entrance from the main road has been walled in although the notice remains on the wall. Estate plans and papers, now in the Bristol Records Office, are said to have been kept here.

Members of the Bristol Savages. The group includes in the front row, centre, F.S. Richardson, St Martins (President); Mr H.C. Guyatt, Folleigh Lane (schoolmaster); Mr H.B. Napier, Hobwell House (centre, back row looking to Club House). Mr Napier was Agent for Ashton Court from 1901 until his death in 1932. He was a well-known figure in rustic jacket, knee breeches, long socks and lace-up boots, with his long holly thumb-stick, accompanied by his retriever dog.

Alfred William Stone (1856-1945), photographed by the Hon. Mrs Esmé Smyth. He was born at Fir Tree Cottage (now Well House) and after training in carpentry and architecture, was appointed Clerk of Works to the Ashton Court Estates, becoming Architect in 1902. Projects in which he was involved included work at the Research Station, houses in Glebe Road, the vicar's vestry at the parish church and the Hunting Lodge which now forms the core of Redwood Lodge Country Club.

20

Three
Churches and Chapels

The Domesday survey records the existence of a church here in 1086 but the present parish church, dedicated to All Saints, was built in about 1380 by Thomas de Lyons, Lord of the Manor of Ashton Lyons. During following centuries it has been much altered and probably enlarged. It was restored in 1871-72. The churchyard contains numerous interesting tombs and a Churchyard Trust was set up in 1994 to preserve, maintain and repair them. In the eighteenth century, Elizabeth Hodges became companion to Mrs Weare of Ashton Lodge. Elizabeth, who belonged to the Castle Green congregation in Bristol, bore witness to her beliefs and a group of people began to meet in a cottage for worship. In 1792, Mr John Fisher Weare purchased part of an orchard near Clarkencombe and built the first Congregational chapel. Nonconformists were meeting for worship in cottages at Providence in 1834. They may have built the 'Chapel of the Brethren', which existed by 1881 and continued in use until after the Second World War. Hebron Evangelical Church was built in Providence Lane, in 1934.

Interior, before the Restoration. — Aug 13. 1871.
Photo' the day they began it, by pulling down the Old Gallery (Thatched.)

The caption on this photograph was written by Avena Blackburne. The panels on the chancel wall, bearing the Ten Commandments, were erected in 1694, later covered and revealed again in the 1840s. The tops of the Smyth pews in the north chapel can just be seen. By 1849, the decorated sounding board above the three-decker pulpit had been removed.

Church interior in the 1930s. The chancel was completely rebuilt in 1871-72 and a new organ was installed in the south chapel. The dark pine pews were set on a three-inch plinth and enclosed the pillars, leaving only a very narrow passageway in the aisles. In the foreground is part of the Victorian font. The Decalogue, Apostles' Creed and Lord's Prayer were put up on the east wall in 1893.

The Old Vicarage. There was a vicarage here by 1446, opposite a close called Le Sperte. Rev John Collinson, vicar from 1787-93, published his three-volume *History of Somerset* while he lived here. It was in such a ruinous state that, in October 1798, it was demolished and immediately rebuilt. In 1883 it ceased to be a vicarage and became a private house called The Glebe. It is now Lampton House retirement home.

The Vicarage and church in the early 1900s. In the nineteenth century, a Georgian building called Merriott's Lodge was occupied by a wine merchant, Sidney Grey Bees. He surrendered his lease in 1883 and it became the new vicarage, a few months before Rev Blackburne's death. The building was made uninhabitable by enemy action in January 1941.

Rev John E. Varley, vicar from 1919-35, with his wife and son outside the Vicarage in September 1923.

Rev G.R. Blackburne in the driving seat, Mrs Blackburne, Avena Blackburne, Hannah Hough (maid), Ephraim Michael (groom), Chessie and Beeswax. Rev Gilbert Robard Blackburne was vicar of Long Ashton from 1841 until his death in 1883. His grave is shown in the next photograph. The restoration of the church took place during his incumbency and services were held in the Parochial Schools. The church was rededicated on 13 August 1872.

Tomb of Rev Blackburne and his wife with the Church Cross in the background. There were once seven crosses in the parish but now only part of Church Cross remains. In 1495 the Cross stood next to the Angel Inn but in 1882 it was moved to the churchyard, near Parsonage Farm wall, at Sir Greville Smyth's expense. It must have been moved again to its present position in the churchyard after the south boundary wall was demolished in 1894-95 to allow for extensions.

Part of the choir in 1871 (trebles and altos). Avena Blackburne is in the back row, second from left.

Mothers' Union outing to Cheddar, 1 September, 1921. Among those in the party were Mrs Kempe (St Martins) and Mrs Harding (Jessamine Cottage). The coach was Bristol Tramways and Carriage Co. No. 35, built at the Carriage Works, Brislington.

Some of the All Saints' Church bell-ringers who rang to celebrate VE Day, 8 May 1945. From left to right, back row: Frank Bridle, Percy Yeo, Paul Duggett, Peter Faux. Front row: George Yeo (Captain), Ruth Knight, David Yeo. In front of Ruth is David Bridle.

Three generations of bell ringers – David Yeo, Percy Yeo, George Yeo – November 1948.

Volunteers at work in the Church in 1948. On the left, Mr Thomas, the verger, helps to clean the nave while the vicar, Rev Hugh Knapman, steadies the ladder. Kenneth Escott is climbing the scaffolding. The medieval font in the foreground was discovered by the vicar being used as a flowerpot in the garden of Parsonage Farm. It was given back to the church and was rededicated on All Saints' Day 1940.

More volunteers help to refurbish All Saints' Church in 1948. From left to right: Mrs Bloyce, Maud Escott and Ruth Knight are altering the seat runners for the pews. Ron Chorley (standing) and Eric Hobbis are stripping the pews to their natural colour and reducing their size in order to make wider passageways in the aisles.

Lady Smyth laying the foundation stone of St Mary's, Leigh Woods on 1 August 1891. The development of Leigh Woods in the nineteenth century and its distance from the parish church at Long Ashton, made the provision of a new church to serve the settlement, a pressing need. Clergy present at the ceremony included Bishop Cheetham, Dean of Wells and Rev Hugh Falloon of Long Ashton. The choristers came from Long Ashton, Ashton Gate and Flax Bourton.

St Mary's, Leigh Woods was completed by October 1892 and licensed for worship. The Leigh Woods Land Company had granted the site free of charge. Mr John Medland was the architect and Messrs R. Wilkins & Sons, the builders. Nearly £4,000 was raised towards the cost and numerous gifts helped to furnish and equip the building. A new ecclesiastical district of Leigh Woods was defined, within the Bath and Wells diocese. Assistant Bishop Bromby consecrated the church on 18 October 1893.

The lychgate, St Mary's, Leigh Woods, is a memorial to those who died in the First World War. A replica of the gate has since been erected in the garden of remembrance in Long Ashton Church burial ground.

The choir, vicar and churchwardens, St Mary's, Leigh Woods, September 1911. The vicar, from 1892 to 1922, was Rev Canon John Gamble. The two churchwardens were Mr George (later Sir George) Wills of Burwalls and Mr J.N.C. Pope. The choirboys, from the Ashton Gate district, were granted the Agnes Bromby scholarship if they attended regularly. Agnes was the daughter of Bishop Bromby and a former choir-mistress. In 1976, St Mary's combined with Holy Trinity, Abbots Leigh and is now in the Bristol diocese.

The choir and minister of the Congregational church, *c.* 1900. From left to right, back row: Dorothy Hicks, girl from Clifton, Mr Newman Jnr, Mr Newman Snr, Mr Hicks, girl from Clifton, Ann Burges. Front row: Dorothy Newman, Clair Durston, Letty Barnes, Mr Claridge (minister), Miss Baker (organist), Miss Milson, Gladys Childe. In front are Mr Newman Jnr and Jilly Rossiter. The church, now the United Reform Church, was erected in 1892, one hundred years after a chapel had been built near Clarkencombe.

Providence Chapel, the day after it was destroyed by fire, 26 November 1928. When this chapel was built, and by whom, is not known, but it was sold to lay preachers by the Smyth Estate in 1921 for the use of the Brethren, an independent denomination. The chapel was rebuilt after the fire. When the Brethren ceased to use it, the Scouts met there and eventually purchased the building, opening it as their HQ on 24 August 1957.

Ernest Dyer came to Long Ashton in 1912 to take a boys' Sunday school class at Providence Chapel. In 1920, he assumed full responsibility for the work there. After the chapel had been rebuilt, following the fire in 1928, there were disagreements among the congregation as to how the work should continue. Mr Dyer and others began to hold services in the Unionist Hall. This was the beginning of the Evangelical Christian Church in Long Ashton. When Hebron Evangelical Church was built in 1934, Mr Dyer became Sunday school superintendent, youth leader, choirmaster and organist. He rose at 5am and spent two hours in prayer and Bible study. From the age of fourteen until his retirement, he worked for J.S. Fry & Sons, where he founded a United Christian fellowship. During the evenings he conducted mid-week services at the church, arranged church business and did visiting. On Saturday afternoons and evenings, he prepared his sermons. He died in September 1967, aged 73.

Original exterior of Hebron Evangelical Church, Providence Lane. The building opened on 7 October 1934, on land obtained from the Ashton Court Estate. Originally the entrance was at the side and a front entrance was added later. The church was first owned by Ernest Dyer but later, a trust deed was drawn up to release the ownership. The Dyer family and later, Mr Dyer's sister, Florence, were given life-long occupancy of the flat which had been incorporated in the new building.

Original interior, Hebron Evangelical Church, Providence Lane.

Four

Schools

A cottage near the church was known as School House from 1644. Both Francis Derrick in 1661 and Mrs Anne Smyth in 1760, left bequests for teaching poor children, which were administered by the church. In 1818, the first Parochial School was built with the aid of a grant of £75 from the National Society and other bequests. It was replaced by a new school in Long Ashton Road in 1861. This too was a National School, but open to children of all denominations. It is now Northleaze VC Primary School. For some years, nonconformists also had a school on Providence, established in 1884 with the aid of the British Society. A second primary school was opened at Birdwell in 1967. There were many private schools in Long Ashton from the eighteenth to the present century; some were just dame schools while others offered a good standard of education. The earliest on record was opened by Nathaniel Ainsworth at Ashton Watering (Gatcombe) in 1754. Several of these private schools were situated at or near Westleaze, the area running from Milverton House to the lane by Bourton Mead.

Tomb of Mr John Kempe (Churchwarden.) Erected by Pupils & Parishioners.

This photograph, from Avena Blackburne's album, shows John Kempe (inset), who purchased Thomas Husband's 'Westleaze House Establishment for Young Gentlemen' in 1845. He moved to St Martins c. 1851. Long Ashton School offered a good education and produced some fine cricketers including E.M. Grace and Alfred Grace, two of W.G. Grace's brothers. John Kempe died on 16 April 1874, aged 60.

W.J. Kempe's school, Long Ashton, August 1880. Wilfred John Kempe continued to run the school after his father's death until c. 1914. He died in 1915, aged 65. When this photograph was taken, there were about seventy boarders at the school, a large number of them coming from South Wales.

St Martin's Cottage. When Nathaniel Ainsworth leased the property from Sir Jarrit Smith on 29 September 1769, it was known as 'Jordan's' or 'West Crouders Yeat'. John Kempe leased it from Ashton Court Estate in 1850-51 and eventually it became the infirmary and an additional dormitory for his school. Brigadier-General R.E.H. Dyer, who ordered the shooting at Amritsar in 1919, retired to the cottage in 1926. He died on 11 July 1927. His wife continued to live there for some years.

Westleaze School, Ivy Cottage, 1896. From left to right, back row: Edith Perry (Hill House); Mabel Shore (main road); Harriet Marshall; Amy Hicks. Third row: Kathleen Stone (Glen View); Elsie Gill (Fir Tree Cottage); Miss Lukins (teacher, Ivy Cottage). Second row: Roy Bignell; Rene Gill (Fir Tree Cottage); Mollie Stone (Glen View); ? Marshall (Yanley Lane). Front row: ? Marshall (Yanley Farm); -?-; Cyril Gill (Fir Tree Cottage).

The Grange, 1907. Mrs Emily Hobdell, who in 1858 was running a school for young ladies at Westleaze House, moved to The Grange between 1861 and 1862. After Mrs Hobdell's death, Miss Eliza Reeves opened her school here 'for a select number of young ladies' from September 1864 until her death in 1876. When this photograph was taken, William Perry was living in The Grange.

Miss Snow's school at Church House in the 1920s. From left to right: Howard Valentine; -?-; -?-; Jack Valentine (Barn Hey); Peter Prideaux (Bowley House); -?-; -?-; Tony Lees; Patrick Richardson (St Martins); Marjorie Verdon-Smith (Hill House).

The Wyck Room, c. 1935. Built behind the almshouses as a mission room in 1898 at a cost of about £134, it was constructed of timber with a galvanised roof. Ashton Court Estate workers undertook the basic work and it was erected by Wrinch & Son. In 1928 it was still used for Sunday school, weekly Bible classes and Children's Guild. The building was demolished in September 1969 and a bungalow now occupies the site.

Pupils at the Wyck Room, *c.* 1935. From 4 May 1918 to 21 December 1961, the Wyck Room was also used as a day school, run by Miss Lilian Webb for pupils aged five to fifteen. From left to right, back row: -?-, Valerie Carey, Miss Webb. Middle row: Colin Maltby, Doris Rattle, Murray Stevens, Dick Clist, -?-, Gordon Harris, -?-, Brian Harris, -?-. Front row: -?-, Roy Harris, -?-, Michael Corrigan, Mary Uppington, Michael Radford, Ruth Knight. In the background are Nos. 92, 90, then 84, 82, Ridgeway Road.

Mrs Milsom and Mrs Lizzie Hazell standing outside the former Parochial School in Church Lane. A master and mistress occupied the teachers' house (shown here) rent-free and received a salary of £17 10s per annum. Behind the house was a schoolroom with accommodation for about fifty pupils. After replacement by a new school in 1861, it became two cottages.

SCHOOL, LONG ASHTON.

Church House and the Parochial Schools, *c.* 1910. The Parochial Schools, on the right, replaced the building in Church Lane. The foundation stone was laid on 12 November 1860. The schools were completed by 1861 at a cost of nearly £2,200 and included cloakrooms and a master's house. The official opening took place on 21 January 1862. Further along the road, the new Church House on the left, was paid for by Lady Smyth in 1907 to replace the former Church House (Angel Inn).

The Girls' department of Long Ashton Parochial School in 1887. Children were then required to hand over 1*d* per week to the school for their education. The headmaster was Henry Coulton Guyatt who had been appointed as an assistant in October 1879. When John Price resigned in June 1880, owing to ill-health, Henry Guyatt became headmaster.

Long Ashton Parochial School in 1902. This seems to be the infants' class. The teacher is on the right in the back row. The pupil, front centre, is O. Kingston.

Woodwork class, Long Ashton Parochial School, 1928. From left to right, back row: G. Anstey, F.N. Hynam, N. Gates, F.W. Hynam, G. Lansbury, Mr H.W. Gunston, J. Barnes, H. Calvey. Front row: B. Barnes, L. Cook, M. Evans, A. Ambrose, S. Lawrence, H. Froud.

An arts and crafts class at the Parochial School in 1932. From left to right: Iris Vine, Jean Smith, Olive Davis, Mr Gunston, Hon. Mrs Esmé Smyth. Mrs Smyth took a keen interest in the school and often taught art, barbola, renasco and glass painting.

School pageant, Ashton Court, July 1932. 220 scholars, aged between five and fourteen, took part. Tiny tots performed a nursery pageant. Despite poor weather, there were two performances. Pupils were trained by the headmaster, Mr W.J. Allen, assisted by Mr B.L. Perrett, Miss Willcox, Mrs Humphrey, Mrs Chalke, Miss Ridd and Miss Kingsland. Shown here are Jack Faulkner (Robert, Earl of Leicester), Betty Fudge, Betty Barnes (Queen Elizabeth I) and Harold Hinder (Sir Walter Raleigh).

Five

Farming and
Market Gardening

In 1805, Shiercliffe's Bristol and Hotwells Guide said this of Long Ashton: 'The land is rich and well-cultivated; abounds in neat cottages and gardens, in which are raised flowers, vegetables, fruit and particularly great quantities of strawberries and raspberries, which are eaten with cream by visitants from the Hotwells and Bristol.' The Strawberry Gardens at Bower Ashton, which were open from about 1818 to 1848, were a special attraction for the visitors, who crossed the river by way of the Rownham ferry. Up to the 1930s, strawberries for the Bristol market were grown in large quantities on the south-facing slopes of the village. Market gardening was an important occupation and there were about a dozen market gardens in Long Ashton in the 1920s. There is still one today, which grows bedding plants. Today there are still several working farms in the parish and fields come close to the road, especially on the south side of the village. Some of the old field names, like Westleaze, Northleaze and Parsonage Close, have been revived when naming the new built-up areas of the village.

Haymaking at Lower Court Farm in the 1890s. Thomas Henry Pearce was then the farmer at Lower Court.

The North Somerset Show at Ashton Court, 1881. Jersey cow 'Bramble' won first prize. The first show may have been staged at Yatton in 1856. It was then held at several other venues in the locality but for many years now, the show has taken place at Ashton Court.

Mr Milsom, head cowman at Home Farm, Bower Ashton. The photograph was taken by the Hon. Mrs Esmé Irby (later Smyth).

Mrs Lucy Yeo, Percy Yeo (centre) and George Yeo in their market garden in 1907. The original Lampton House, on the left, is named after Lamington or Lampton, one of the original settlements. Next-door is the Bird-in-Hand public house, with Laburnam Terrace on the right. George Yeo came to Long Ashton from Devon in 1886, aged 17. After he married, he began his market garden. In 1961, the land was sold for a housing development which was named Yeomeads after the family.

Phil Patch and two others with binder and horses.

Haymaking at the Research Station, during the First World War.

Bringing home the hay. From left to right: Doris Griffiths, Dickie Dingle, Charlie Ward, Frank Bridle and Len Williams standing on top of the hay. The photograph shows the left-hand side of Glebe Road before its development.

Lower Court Farm in 1939. The carter is Mr Wilson of Mill Cottages, whose family was killed by enemy action during the Second World War.

Backing a horse and cart out of the rickyard at Gatcombe Farm, in the 1930s, after unloading hay.

THE "GATCOMBE" SALE
OF
48
Attested
DAIRY SHORTHORNS

WEDNESDAY, 23rd NOVEMBER, 1955
at 12 noon

Owners :	Auctioneers :
Mr. J. H. and Exors. of late Mrs. E. M. BUTLER	R. B. TAYLOR & SONS
Gatcombe Farm	16 Princes Street
FLAX BOURTON	YEOVIL
Bristol	Somerset

Front cover of a catalogue for a sale of dairy shorthorns at Gatcombe Farm in 1955. Gatcombe did not come into the Smyth family's hands until the 1840s. When the farm was auctioned in 1948, along with other parts of the Ashton Court Estate, it was described as 'a double-fronted stone and pantiled Gentleman's farm house'.

Queuing for a haircut from a travelling hairdresser at Gatcombe Farm *c.* 1947, with Henry Butler in the foreground.

Martin Jones followed by John Butler and his son, Henry, drilling corn in the field beyond the railway, Gatcombe Farm. The photograph was taken looking towards Barrow. The bypass now runs across the top of the field.

When the railway cutting was being dug out in 1838, remains of Roman buildings were uncovered at Gatcombe. In August 1954, the Clevedon Archaeological Society carried out excavations at the farm, after John Butler found Roman coins and farm animals had uncovered part of a wall. Here, in the cider orchard, John Butler (extreme left) is holding part of a carved altar slab. His wife Edith (extreme right) watches an archaeologist at work.

John Butler and his wife during the 1954 excavations. Archaeologists from Bristol University carried out regular excavations on the site during the 1960s and 1970s, uncovering the remains of a large Roman settlement. These were later covered over to preserve them.

Six

Shops

The first shop in Long Ashton to be well authenticated is that of John Howard, the butcher. It stood on the site of the garden at Sunnymead, opposite the Angel Inn. Howard moved there in 1730 and was followed by his eldest son Henry, also a butcher, in 1769. John Morgan, who lived at this house after the Howards, was described as a shopkeeper but what he sold is not recorded. Directories show that, by the 1850s, Long Ashton had a post office, bakery, at least one butcher and several grocers and tea-dealers. Chorley's stores had been established at Birdwell by 1871. By the late 1920s and early 1930s, more shops had opened throughout the village, although mostly at the western end, which was steadily developing. Nowadays, the shops, including the post office, are nearly all concentrated in the Birdwell area of Long Ashton. Some have altered completely, and now include two dentists, two estate agents and a library. As in so many towns and villages today, local shops have to compete with large supermarkets in the locality. Sadly, several shops have closed, reverting to private use, and more are under threat.

The Ellicott family, Long Ashton Stores, c. 1896. Shown are Arthur Ellicott and his wife Mary (seated, centre) with their children, Joseph Edward, Mary Annett, William Arthur, Arthur, Millicent Annie and Bertha Alice. William later became an amateur astronomer.

Arthur Ellicott, Mrs Ellicott and Bertha, their daughter, standing outside the Village Stores, *c*. 1900. Arthur Ellicott was proprietor of the stores from *c*. 1881 to 1909 and sold beer and groceries, but he was a proficient house-carpenter by trade.

Beaufort Cottage, on the corner of Baker's Lane (now Folleigh Lane) and Long Ashton Road, in August 1880. This was the first village post office. A time signal was sent through to the postmaster each day so that villagers could set their clocks accurately. Albert John Poultney had assisted his father, John, as telegraph and postman's clerk, then succeeded him in 1878. He was a corn and seed merchant as well as being postmaster.

Arthur Newman, postman, and Miss Emily Nurse, sub-postmistress, standing outside the third post office, *c.* 1911. The post office had transferred to No. 102 Long Ashton Road by about 1896. Later it moved to these new premises by the Ashton Arms public house. Miss Nurse also sold stationary. Arthur Edwin Newman lived in Linden Cottage, Short Lane (now Hillside Road) where, from 1907, he ran the first telephone exchange in Long Ashton. In 1912 he moved to Rose Cottage, Hobwell Lane.

Eliza Chorley began the shop which traded at Birdwell for about a hundred years. Her husband was a house-carpenter. Eliza borrowed £10 and sold paraffin from a hand-cart before opening the shop.

Harry Chorley and helpers with 'Tom' the horse, outside their shop. Harry was Eliza's son. Groceries were delivered by a horse-drawn van until a motor-van was acquired in 1919.

Harry Chorley, Hannah, his wife, and their children, Albert, Elsie and Percy. Albert, Eliza's grandson, was later to become senior partner in the business with his brother, Percy.

Albert and Elsie Chorley in Keed's Lane, *c.* 1909.

Chorley's shop (*see page 51*). There used to be open fields between the shop and the Robin Hood's Retreat public house on Providence Lane. The shop traded from 8am to 10pm and Albert Chorley once recollected that he did not have a holiday until he was an adult.

Butcher's shop, Chestnut Farm (opposite Church House) before the Second World War. From left to right: Alf Richards, Bert Dallin, W.E. James. Ernest B. James was the farmer at Chestnut Farm. A dairy and a butcher's shop were attached to the farm. The shop was let, then lay empty until Mr W.E. James reopened it in the 1920s. It was closed by 1976.

James' butcher's shop, Birdwell, c. 1951. From left to right: Fred Grindle, Jeff Ives, W.E. James, Fred Hynam. This end of the village was then expanding and Mr W.E. James opened a second butcher's shop here, where Taylor's once had been.

Looking from H.J. Taylor's butcher's shop (now James's) to the Bird-in-Hand public house in the early 1930s. The sign reads 'H.J. Taylor. Family Butcher. Open Daily. And at Hotwells.' No. 49 – private house. No. 47 – built in 1926 (Mrs Jessie Gregory sold confectionery and may be the person at the gate). No. 45 – Mr W.J. James, groceries and general store; his name is also on the side of the building. A sign near the shop reads 'Refreshments. Players Navy Cut Cigarettes.' The sign by the pavement reads 'Gentlemen's Hairdressing Saloon, Side Entrance.' Mr T. Frampton, hairdresser, had a room at the rear. No. 43 – Miss M. Bryant and Miss V. Bryant, aunt and niece, ran a draper's and haberdashery business. The area beyond the private houses was occupied by a yard and stables. A small business was run from a shed, where sticks were chopped, then delivered. Greenland, Bast and Yates, builders used the ground floor of the large two-storey building while Avon Radio Manufacturing Co. made wireless accessories upstairs. The sign on the side of the Bird-in-Hand advertises Newberry's Furniture.

Birdwell, looking west, from the chemist's to the Gardeners Arms public house, 1938. Shops now occupy the site of the yard and stables. George Knight's chemist's shop is out of the picture but a sign on the pavement advertises 'Ucal Products'. Next door, Cyril Parsons sells sweets, tobacco and newspapers. The newspaper boards may be referring to the Munich Crisis – 'A Grim Scrap Of Paper'. Next comes Charles Henry Hunt's grocer's shop and finally H.J. Taylor, who had now opened a shop here.

Panes' Store, decorated for the Coronation of King George VI in 1937. The shop was run by Reginald and Roland Panes as Panes Bros. Grocers.

Seven

Public Houses

The Angel Inn was originally the Church House, granted to trustees in 1495 by Sir John Choke. Parish meetings were held there and travellers could obtain refreshments. From 1553, it formed part of Moryces Charity, to be used for the benefit of the church and poor of Long Ashton. In the early eighteenth century it became known as the Angel Inn. An ancient court, the Court Leet, met there to deal with petty offences and, according to tradition, magistrates' courts were also held there. The cellars were once the village lock-up. It remained the Church House until 1902. The Smyth Arms was originally a cottage at Bower Ashton. It became an alehouse, with a somewhat unsavoury reputation, during the sixteenth century. First named the Coach and Horses, it was renamed the Smyth Arms in the 1860s, after the owners of the estate. The Court Leet sometimes met there. When the turnpike road was built, it became a coaching inn. The Bird-in-Hand was very popular with Bristol visitors in the 1890s and a row of brakes was often drawn up outside. The Miners Rest at Providence began as a cottage where miners and quarrymen could get refreshments. The Robin Hood's Retreat, a short distance away, was originally two cottages.

Mrs Emma Brown and three of her children, outside the Smyth Arms, c. 1878. Edward Brown was landlord of the Smyth Arms from c. 1860 to 1890. The inn was part of the Smyth Estate and was sold to Georges Brewery in 1948.

The Angel Inn, *c.* 1860. The first recorded landlord, in 1597, was Richard Addys. Although still the Church House, by the eighteenth century it had become a popular hostelry known as the Angel Inn. Young men took part in contests of backsword or butt and cudgel, to try to win money, a fine beaver hat or a pair of buckskin breeches. Church Cross stood outside the inn until 1882. The stocks and whipping post still remained in the lane beside the inn in 1829.

Samuel Edward ('Teddy') Evans, the landlord from 1908 to 1923, standing at the entrance to the Angel Inn.

Mr and Mrs Gray at the bar of the Angel Inn. The Ashton Gate Brewery leased the inn in 1914. George Gray was landlord from 1949 to 1959 and his wife, Mrs Mary Gray held the licence, after her husband's death, until about 1967. When Georges Brewery took over in the 1960s, a six-day licence was still in force but Mrs Gray succeeded in having it extended to seven days a week.

The Bird-in-Hand. The name of the landlady, Mrs Fanny Burnett, appears on the side of the building. She was licensee from c. 1905 to 1916. In the late nineteenth century, a horse-drawn bus ran between the Bird and the Talbot public house in Redcliffe Street, Bristol, making two journeys Mondays, Tuesdays, Wednesdays, and Fridays, and three journeys on Thursdays and Saturdays. The fare to Ashton Gate was about 2d and to Bristol, 4d. Later, another operator introduced a rival service.

Bert Edwards, Len Kingston and Mollie Edwards in the Ashton Arms. Bert and Mollie Edwards were the landlord and landlady for over 20 years. Bill and Elsie Wine, who succeeded them, had been at the Ashton Arms for less than a year when it closed in October 1966.

Mrs Phil Patch, family and friends standing outside the Gardeners Arms. From left to right: Willie Patch, Lizzie Patch (sister of Willie), Percy Patch, Edna Patch, Mrs Patch and two customers. Mrs Rosina Patch was licensee by 1935. The Gardeners Arms, which stood on the corner of Weston Road and Birdwell Road, was closed in the 1950s. It was demolished when new premises were built for a Gateway supermarket in 1971.

Eight
Village Activities

A century ago, facilities at the Working Men's Club – known as the Village Club – included billiards, skittles and a small library. Bible classes for men and women and mothers' meetings were also held there each week. There was a weekly singing class for young ladies and the County Education Committee sponsored lectures on topics like domestic science, beekeeping and health education. The club also arranged flower shows in Ashton Park. Nowadays, there are numerous clubs and societies in the village catering for a wide range of interests and ages including arts and crafts, bingo, conservation, dancing, drama, local history, yoga, a whist club and wildlife, together with social and fund-raising organisations like the Royal British Legion and the WI. Other groups cater for younger villagers, such as Scouts, Guides, the Duke of Edinburgh Award scheme and the youth club, which offers judo, gymnastics and a Saturday morning cinema club. Age Concern provides a day centre for the elderly, the Good Companions Club meets each week and LACCA (Long Ashton Area Community Care Amenities) offers practical support for the sick and elderly.

The Village Club which was erected in 1878 at the foot of Providence on Ashton Court Estate land. It had a meeting-room, billiards-room and small flat for the caretaker. The club was open to residents aged 18 and over. Sir Greville Smyth officially let the building to three trustees in 1885 although it was in use by February 1879. The nominal rent was 3d per quarter.

Mrs Jefferies presenting the British Legion banner to T. Crewe and W. French. Also in the picture are Major Paterson, L. Clist, B. Worral (the last Agent to Ashton Court) and B. Hynam. The local branch of the British Legion was formed in 1936 at an inaugural meeting of over 200 people, held at Church House. The branch made an arrangement with the Working Men's Village Club to use the premises as its headquarters. When the Hon. Mrs Esmé Smyth died in 1946 and the estates sold off, the Village Club was unable to raise the money to purchase the clubhouse which had been acquired by Newcombe Estates. The British Legion later bought the premises from the company in 1949, for £2,250, and guaranteed that those who would have been eligible for Village Club membership would still be admitted.

Mary Rooke in 1926 when she was Long Ashton Guide Captain. She married Captain A.F. Harding MC, the future Lord Harding of Petherton, at All Saints' Church on 21 April 1927. Guides from Long Ashton and Flax Bourton formed a guard of honour. (*See page 91*)

Group of Guides, 1944. Shown are Avis Conn, Joy Maggs, Bridget Uppington, Peggy Clark, Angela Ware, Margo Davis, Margaret Sherborne, Sheila Anstey, Vera Rossiter, Doreen Maggs, Betty Lewis, Margaret Harris, Barbara Hynam, Diane Willmot, Phyllis Searle, Pauline Chorley.

Presentation at Long Ashton Flower Show in the 1930s. From left to right: Harold Patch, Percy
King, Percy Yeo, Mrs Harrington Fry, Charlie Tucker, Harry Connock, George Childs. A
flower show was held in Ashton Park from about 1880 to 1893 but folded, apparently through
lack of support. In February 1919, the Long Ashton Horticultural Society was formed. Until
1928, shows were held in Ashton Park in conjunction with the North Somerset Agricultural
Society. They moved first to the Recreation Ground at Keedwell and then to the old Village
Hall. The Society lapsed during the Second World War but resumed in 1946.

Women's Institute Garden Party at Ashover in 1947. Mrs Kingston, who lived at Ashover, is on the right, sitting down, third row from the front. The Long Ashton Branch of the WI held its first committee meeting on 27 January 1930. Mrs Napier was in the Chair, Mrs Richardson and Mrs Valentine were elected Vice-Presidents, Mrs Kingston as Treasurer, Mrs Ridd as Secretary and Mrs Stenner as Assistant Secretary.

Members of the WI invited their menfolk to the annual party and entertainment in 1945 and the men reciprocated. At a meeting, it was agreed to make use of the talent in the village by staging a pantomime. In 1947 *Aladdin* was presented by the Village Voices, named after the Village Association's newsletter. In the centre of the photograph is Harold Smith, who wrote and produced the pantomime, together with some of the cast and others involved in the production.

Jack and the Beanstalk, 1950. Following the success of *Aladdin*, the Panto Club was formed in 1948. Their first production was *Cinderella*, followed by *Robinson Crusoe* in 1949. *Jack and the Beanstalk* was written and produced by Bernard Low. The cast included Judy Hurley as Fairy Cretonia, Jo Williams as Jack and Don Mereweather as Mrs Painter (Jack's mother). By 1959, productions like these had been affected by the impact of television and the club lay dormant.

The Good Old Days produced by the Village Association in the old Village Hall, *c.* 1958. The Village Association arranged numerous activities to raise money to improve village amenities and towards the cost of building the new Village Hall which opened on 14 November 1959.

Nine
Sport and Recreation

Long Ashton has always had a number of clubs and facilities for those interested in sport. The Cricket Club, which now meets near Yanley Lane, originated in the last century, as did the Golf Club, some years later. Today, there is a much more varied choice of sports activities. A second golf club opened a few years ago, at Yanley Lane. The Rifle Club meets on the Weston Road. There is a football pitch on the Recreation Ground, with both senior and junior clubs. During the outdoor season, the Bowling Club meets at Keedwell Hill and in winter, plays short-mat bowls in the Village Hall. The Tennis Club uses the courts on Keedwell Hill while at the Recreation Ground are a children's play area, a fenced area for young children, skateboard ramp, and a hard-surface five-a-side football and basketball area. The Badminton Club meets in the nearby Sports Hall where basketball is also played. The facilities at the Recreation Ground and Sports Hall are managed by the Long Ashton Community Association.

Cricket ground, 1872. In March 1856, the Cricket Club met on the field near the church and afterwards dined at the Angel Inn. In a match on 18 July 1857, the home team included Tom Dyke, E.M. Grace, J.H.G. Smith and Rev Blackburne. At a sports meeting here on 26 May 1866, E.M. Grace won two events whilst W.G. Grace won three.

A cricket match taking place in the field opposite Ashover in 1880. Miss Avena Blackburne (left) and Florence Stock are two of the spectators. Rings were fixed in the wall so that an iron ladder could be erected to give access to the field. Tithes were once an important source of church income and in the background is the medieval tithe barn. Its original roof was destroyed by fire in June 1966.

Cricket Club in the 1890s. Shown are A.J. Welsby, F. Cobbett, H. Guyatt, J. Hicks Burrington Ham, ? Tycke. The club folded in 1883 after it had proved too difficult to persuade residents to play and subscriptions were in arrears. However, as a result of a meeting held at the Angel Inn in October 1883, a new club was rapidly formed. In November, a committee reported on the laying-out of a new ground after Sir Greville Smyth provided five acres, rent-free, in 'Mr Wookey's field', off Yanley Lane.

Cricket Club, 1906. From left to right, back row: Stuart Kempe, Stanley Pearce, Bill Harvey, Jack Perry, Edgar Pearce, Mr Fisher, Bill Smith, Fred Perry, Martin Chart. Middle row: W.P. Kingston, Bert Watts, William Perry Snr, Rev Deering (vicar), H.W. Gunston, Mr Smith, Bill Herd, Harry Perry, Waff Walker. In front, H.W. Guyatt is on the left.

Cricket Club (1st XI), 1925. From left to right, back row: A. Watts, H.W. Gunston, A. Evans, L. Hosegood, W. Smith, H. Kingston, H. Ball, J. Hunt, J. Ball. Front row: G. Yates, C. Leach, C. Organ, G.C. Gunston, F. Organ, J. Barwell, T.T.V. Morgan.

Long Ashton Rangers AFC, Ascott Cup Winners, 1922-23. From left to right, back row: Anstey, Butler, Tucker, Read, L. Poole, Smart, C. Blackmore, A. Williams, W. Stenner, Ratcliffe, W. Blackmore, O. Oatway. Middle row (seated): R. Small, H. Burge, J. Anstey, Ratcliffe, R. Lamb. In front: A. Hynam, A. Butler. The club was formed in 1904, using a field behind the church. It lapsed in 1927, re-forming in 1929, with matches being played on fields behind Wild Country Lane and, later, on the Recreation Ground.

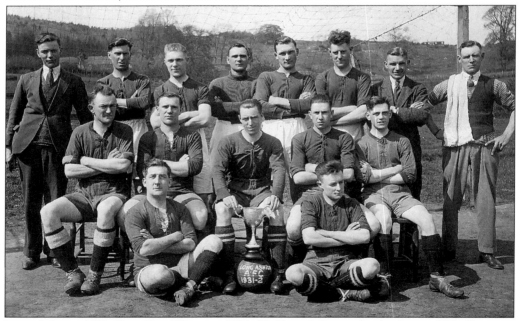

Long Ashton AFC, Pine Cup Winners, 1931-32. From left to right, back row: W.J. Kingston (Hon. Secretary), H. Anstey (Captain), L. Ball (Vice-Captain), A. Kingston, A. Marshall, L. Poole, A. Lewis (Trainer), H. Poole (Assistant Trainer). Middle row: F. Brown, H. Harvey, Len Poole, R. Eamer, G. Lewis. In front: J. Greenland (Treasurer), A. Williams.

Long Ashton Golf Clubhouse, *c.* 1908. The club was formed on 20 November 1893 when seven people met at Wilfred Kempe's house in St Martins. Sir Greville Smyth allowed the club to use land on the hill above Folleigh Lane, during winter months only, free of charge – Richmond Harding, a local farmer, used the land for grazing cattle and horses during the summer. Sir Greville Smyth was the first President and William Kempe was Captain from 1894 to 1897. The original clubhouse was made of galvanised iron and cost about £20 when it was erected in 1895-96. It was enlarged in November 1899. The building in the photograph was erected in 1906 and became a private residence in 1938 when the present clubhouse was built on land fronting Failand Road.

Golf Club artisans in the 1920s. From left to right: Harry Hazell, Fred Vowles, Stan Burge, Harold Barnes, -?-, Albert Ball.

Hockey Club 2nd XI, 1951-52. From left to right, back row: P. Wemys, B. Huish, W. Short, J. Wills, R. Holden. Middle row: P.C. Berrill, ? Jenkins, R.A. Woolley. Front row: B. Price, D. Silvester, J. Molton. The club was founded in 1902 with Lady Smyth as President. It lapsed during the First World War and then re-formed. The club folded again when war broke out in 1939. There were difficulties in re-forming the club after the war but it prospered after merging with the South Bristol Hockey Club.

Ten
The Research Station

Successful experiments to improve cider quality at Butleigh Court, near Glastonbury, led to the establishment of a permanent institute for research into cider-making and fruit growing. In 1902, a site was chosen at Fenswood, Long Ashton and the following year the National Fruit and Cider Institute became a limited company. In 1912, the NFCI became associated with the University of Bristol and was known as the Agricultural and Horticultural Research Station although kept its corporate identity. NFCI assets were transferred to the University, which purchased the 257 acres at Fenswood Farm, the original premises of the Institute, and built new laboratories and a cider-house extension. Between 1914 and 1918, new developments in food production replaced much of the research. Cider-apple jelly was produced in 1917. Cider pomace, from which juice had been extracted, proved a valuable source of pectin for jam-making. During the Second World War, blackcurrant syrup and rosehip syrup were developed for the Ministry of Health. Methods of preventing wastage from heavy crops, pest control and soil nutrients, were investigated. The Pomology and Fruit and Beverages Divisions, which had made major contributions to cider and fruit production and research, were wound up in the 1980s but work on crop protection and plant sciences continued.

The National Fruit and Cider Institute, 1904. The laboratory is on the right; the mill-house and apple loft are to the left. The site was leased from the Ashton Court Estate and Lady Smyth offered a loan of £500 towards the cost of converting and improving the buildings. By 1904, alterations had been made to the buildings to provide a mill-house, cellar, stores and a lean-to laboratory.

The Fruit and Cider Institute, *c*. 1930. The large brick building on the corner of Wild Country Lane and Weston Road was the Cider House. When cut-backs led to restructuring of the station in the 1980s, the Cider House was kept open by increasing sales of cider and perry to the public. Then, for a time, a private company, Long Ashton Cider Ltd, traded from the premises. The building now houses the Apple Tree Children's Day Nursery.

The first orchards of cider apple trees and perry pear trees were established in 1904 on a four to five-acre site extending from Weston Road to the ridge adjoining the railway fence. A nursery was established to grow trees for trial orchards. By 1907, soft fruits had been introduced.

Portrait of Professor B.T.P. Barker, Director, 1904-63, painted by James Gunn RA, in 1943. B.T.P. Barker, a Cambridge microbiologist specializing in yeast research, acted as a consultant in the early part of 1904. His expertise was needed to give advice on fermentation studies. He moved to Long Ashton in July 1904 and became Assistant (Resident) Director. Barker was appointed Director of the Institute in 1906 and, later, when the NFCI became associated with the University of Bristol, he became Professor of Agricultural Biology. One of the laboratories at the Research Station is now called the Barker Laboratory.

Trainees in horticulture at the Research Station in 1917.

Mr George Spinks, plant-breeder, in 1924. He is shown cross-fertilizing apple-blossoms in order to obtain new varieties of apples. The blossoms are enclosed in paper bags to prevent accidental cross-fertilization by bees and other insects.

Cider-making, *c*. 1927. From left to right, back row: Eldred Walker ('Man o' Mendip'), E.P. West, B. Hathway. Front row: H. Barnes, Mr Pickford, Otto Groves, C. Cole, L. Durston. E.P. West, personal secretary to Mr Napier, the Agent at Ashton Court Estate, was appointed as part-time correspondent in 1907. He later held the post of Secretary-Manager to the Research Station until 1937.

Storing cider-apples.

Cider-Tasting Day, 5 May 1927. From left to right, back row: Prof. Barker, Mrs Edbrooke, Miss Evans, Mr G.H. Hollingworth (Glos. CC), Mr Frank Burroughs, Mr E.G.F. Walker. Front row: Mr E.P. West, Mr R.J. Hathway, Mr R.J. Pullin, Mr J. Ettle. Annual Tasting Days began in 1906. Cider-tasting competitions were introduced in 1924 and by the 1930s, over 1,000 people attended. Competitions and awards ceased in 1936 and Tasting Days were suspended in 1939. From 1946 to 1977, more formal Sampling Days replaced the pre-war events.

Cider-tasting at the Institute. Shown are Mr H. Locke, John Pullin (cider-maker from Compton-Greenfield), E.P. West, B.T.P. Barker, V.L.S. Charley. Dr Charley began work on the production of blackcurrant syrup in 1936. It was later sold commercially as 'Ribena'.

Hoeing peas, 1945.

Bob Hathway at work in the cider-house in 1957. He began work at the Research Station in 1924 and was cider-maker there for 41 years.

Women Land Workers at the Research Station in the late 1940s. From left to right: Mesdames Stenner, Escott, Hurdle, Ford and Weeks.

Domestic food preservation. Work began in the 1920s to find reliable ways of preserving food and advice on this was passed on by means of courses, advisory work and leaflets. Miss Sturdy is shown at work, bottling pork, in 1954.

Eleven
The Village in Wartime

In 1914, local Territorials, belonging to the 1st Wessex Royal Engineers, went straight from camp at Christchurch to France. Horses were requisitioned to pull gun-carriages and Army mules were kept on the hill at Yanley. Other villagers joined up and, altogether, 35 were killed in action. In 1919, a war memorial tablet, stained glass windows and an oak vestibule were erected in All Saints' Church. On 1 and 5 September 1939, 490 evacuees from four London schools arrived in Long Ashton. Ashton Park was requisitioned as a military transit camp and later became the HQ for US Army, Southern Command. ARP wardens and Home Guard and Observer Corps units were formed locally. Bristolians sheltered in Church House during heavy bombing raids on the city but incendiary devices and high explosive bombs often fell in and around the village. Four members of the Wilson family were killed and one died later, following a direct hit on Mill Cottages on Good Friday, 11 April 1941. A plaque in the church commemorates the sad event. Another plaque on the wall of the Garden of Remembrance commemorates the Polish crew of a Halifax bomber which crashed nearby on 23 November 1944. The new Village Hall was erected as a memorial to those villagers who died in both world wars.

Army officers at St Martins during the First World War. From left to right: Noel Kempe, Army Chaplain's Dept. (later, vicar of Flax Bourton, Rector of Yatton and Rural Dean), Bé Kempe, Service Corps (MT), Stuart Kempe, Service Corps (MT).

In 1917, the Hon. Mrs Esmé Smyth put Ashton Court at the disposal of the Red Cross and gave £1,200 towards its conversion into a hospital for convalescent officers. These members of the British Red Cross were photographed at the mansion during the war. From left to right, back row: Mrs Lizzie Williams, Olive Kingston, Edith Barnes, Elsie Kingston. Middle row: Mrs Goscombe, Nurse Stokes, Elsie Tucker. Front row: Mabel Stenner, Ivy Ogbourne.

Soldiers from Ashton Court form the major part of this group which was photographed outside the Congregational church (now URC) during the First World War.

VAD nurses at St Martins during the First World War. A number of VAD nurses helped at the hospital at Ashton Court.

Chorley's shop, 1940. A brick 'blast' wall was built on top of the original front wall to protect the living room from bomb blast.

Entry in ARP warden's post book, Friday 3 January 1941: 'Two HEs at the Vicarage, one incendiary on the Tower and one on the Vestry roof.' Quick action saved All Saints' Church from the incendiaries but the Vicarage was badly damaged. One bomb fell in front of the building and an hour later, a second fell at the rear. Standing in the remains of the garden are Mrs Knapman (vicar's mother) and the curate, Rev Clifford Wigram. The sexton's head shows above the bomb crater.

Home Guard group, 1942. From left to right, front row (seated): Glide, George Stacey, -?-, -?-, Archie Morrish. Middle row (standing): Harold Patch, -?-, -?-, Alfie Sage, Roland French, John Beviss, -?-, Bill Bartlett, Tom Jones, -?- . Back row: -?-, Percy Yeo, -?, -?-, Alf Pollard. The Home Guard Company HQ was at the Research Station. They also used the Club Room at the Village Club, from 1941.

Long Ashton Army Cadet Unit, during the Second World War. From left to right, standing at the rear: Norman Grimstead, Don Irish, -?-, David Barnes, Mervyn Willmott, Ron Oatway, Fred Atherton, John Young, Norman Thresher, Gerald Gregory, Peter Ball, Alan Crew. Standing: Teddy Vining, -?-, -?-, Fred Reynolds, Jeff Ashley, Donald Evans, Kenny Hynam. Seated: Arthur Stenner, Thomas Jones, Gilbert Stacey, Archie Morrish, Leslie Woods, John Morrish. Seated front: Alan Harvey, Harold Prescott, Ivor Beames. When it was fine, they met at the Research Station but on dark evenings or when it was wet, they paraded at the Unionist Hall (old Village Hall).

The back of the NAAFI bakery, Glebe Road, 1944. Amongst those in the group are Joan Poole, Ken Hynam, Billy Ball, Ethel Ambrose, Gwenda Thresher, May Vining, Flo Thomas, Ada Mower.

The Home Guard take the salute as they march along Weston Road during a Victory celebration, *c.* 1945.

The Home Guard assembled for a parade in Ashton Park.

VE Day street party in Birdwell Road, 1945. Amongst those shown in the photograph are Terry Patch, Royston Patch, Les and Ivy Patch, Enid and Beryl Cook, Margaret Harris, John Morgan, Reg Searle, Mr and Mrs Len Searle, Ron Chorley, Mrs Sisley, George and Phil Lewis, Harold Wilmott, Mrs Williams. Part of a rank of air-raid shelters can be seen on the left, behind the group, with the words, 'God Save' on the side.

Children and helpers gathered for a VE party outside the Congregational Church. The minister, Rev Hubert Davies, is on the right, second row from the front.

Twelve
Village Life (II)

By the 1920s, some infilling was taking place along the main road and building had begun at Chestnut Road and Ridgeway Road. More dwellings were being erected further west at sites such as Providence and Rayens Cross Road. Building ceased when war came in 1939 but peace in 1945 brought a growing demand for new homes. Fenswood Road was extended in 1947 and 98 houses were completed in the Keedwell Hill area between 1948 and 1954. Until hot tar was laid, just before the First World War, the roads were very dusty in dry weather and muddy when it was wet. Horses and carts had given way to the motor-car. The A370, ran through the village and, by the 1950s, increasing traffic was causing major problems. The Village Association was formed in 1945 with the object of fostering the goodwill created in wartime and providing amenities for the village. It organised the Festival of Britain celebrations in 1951.

Long Ashton Road, looking towards Church Lodge in 1929. Henry Winter Evans was landlord of the Angel Inn from 1923 to 1947. Sunnymead is on the left (*see page 11*). The sign over the door reads: 'Ashton Gate Beers, Wines & Spirits'.

Further west along the main road near Yanley Lane in the 1930s. Little has changed in 30 years (*see page 14*) but the post office is now shown on the right-hand side of the road.

'Dorchester Castle', GWR locomotive No. 4090, approaches Long Ashton halt in the late 1920s. The halt opened on 20 September 1926 and closed on 6 October 1941. When approached from the village, it was to the right of the railway bridge in Yanley Lane. The platforms were reached by paths leading from the road either side of the bridge. Each platform had a corrugated iron shelter. Tickets could be purchased at Bridge Farm, the Ashton Arms public house and some shops.

Sidney Wilson, Len Barnes and Bayden Hynam, Somerset County Council employees, at work setting in the 'cat's eyes' and marking white lines on the road.

Ashton Lodge in the 1930s. Mary Rooke (*see page* 63) lived here with her mother and stepfather, Mr and Mrs Harrington Fry. The building was described as a mansion house in an 1826 survey. Mr and Mrs Harrington Fry may be the people in the photograph. The house was demolished early in 1964 to make way for the development known as Lodge Drive.

Margaret Rooke (Mary's sister), Mrs C.A. Harrington Fry, Mrs Elsie Richardson and Mrs Ellen Kempe on their way to church.

Ron Chorley, John Bryant and David Yeo outside Chorley's shop in 1938. Ron Chorley took over the business in 1968 and was the last of the family to trade from the Long Ashton premises before moving to Backwell in 1976.

A205.   Recreation Ground. Long Ashton.

The Recreation Ground from the back of Chorley's shop in 1927. Billy Hynam and family and the Poole family pose for the photographer. This was the children's playground, hence the maypole. In the distance, there are newly built houses on the Weston Road. The Gardeners Arms public house can just be seen above the pram.

The maypole on the Recreation Ground.

A series of three photographs forming a panoramic view from Providence Lane westwards towards Fenswood, in 1938. All three are taken from in front of the Robin Hood's Retreat public house. 1) Extreme left, two more upstairs rooms are being built at Hebron Church. Further down the hill are Nos. 102 and 104 Ridgeway Road. The small buildings to the right are a Bristol Waterworks pumping station, There was once an underground reservoir here. The houses in the middle distance are in Rayens Cross Road. Part of the Birdwell Estate is now built on the fields in front of the railway cutting. 2) the field in the foreground belonged to Mr James of Chestnut Farm. Rayens Cross Road is still being developed. Phase 1 ended at Brock's Lane while Phase 2 continued across the junction with Keedwell Hill, ending at Keed's Lane. In this photograph, only Nos. 50 and 52 have been built in Phase 2, on the corner of the junction, while on the left, beyond these, Nos. 67 and 69 have been constructed by Keed's Lane. Beyond these again are allotments and part of Archgrove. The roofs of Birdwell Road show above the houses in the centre of the photograph and some of the Birdwell estate was later built on the fields behind them. The plantations are at Sidelands. Just right of centre is the Gardeners Arms public house, on the corner of Weston Road and Birdwell Road. On the opposite corner is a grocery store run by Mr and Mrs O. Hemmings (now Beaumont Estates). Further along the main road is the Unionist Hall, then used as the Village Hall. 3) The Recreation Ground, with swings, maypole and slide, is in the foreground. Beyond are the line of houses at Archgrove and developments at Fenswood. The large building at Fenswood is the Sunnyside Children's Home which lasted for about sixty years before closing in March 1966. At first, it catered for both boys and girls but later became just a boys' residential home. The Research Station orchards show up clearly in the photograph.

Festival of Britain procession moving along Ridgeway Road, near the junction with Chestnut Road. The opening festivities took place on 5 May 1951. At 2pm at least twelve organisations, including the barrel-organ team, assembled for the procession through the village. After the church bells had been rung, the procession moved off at about 2.30pm. When it reached the Recreation Ground, there was a comic dog show and a display of physical training.

The Panto Club float and the Players' float, Festival of Britain. The procession has now turned into the lane beside the old Village Hall. The cottages in the background are next to what is now The Little Tipple. The Players' float advertises *The Happiest Days of Your Life*, which was performed on 28 and 29 September and 1 October that year. Percy Goodway was the producer.